Sing With Pop Idols!

Evergreen 2

Flying Without Wings 6

Mack The Knife 14

Unchained Melody 11

Yesterday 20

Exclusive distributors:
Music Sales Limited
8/9 Frith Street, London W1D 3JB, England.
Music Sales Pty Limited
120 Rothschild Avenue, Rosebery, NSW 2018, Australia.

Order No. AM974116
ISBN 0-7119-9439-0
This book © Copyright 2002 by Wise Publications

Unauthorised reproduction of any part of this publication by any means including photocopying is an infringement of copyright.

Music engraved by Paul Ewers Music Design
Cover photograph courtesy of London Features International

Printed in the United Kingdom by
Printwise (Haverhill) Limited, Haverhill, Suffolk.

www.musicsales.com

This publication is not authorised for sale in the United States of America and/or Canada

Wise Publications
London/New York/Paris/Sydney/Copenhagen/Berlin/Madrid/Tokyo

Evergreen

Words & Music by Jörgen Elofsson, Per Magnusson & David Kreuger

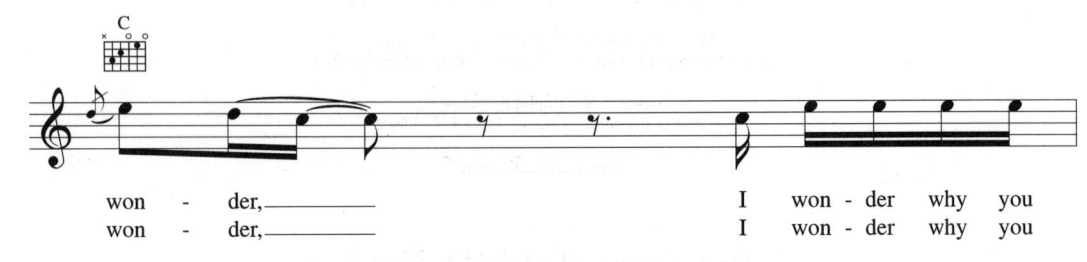

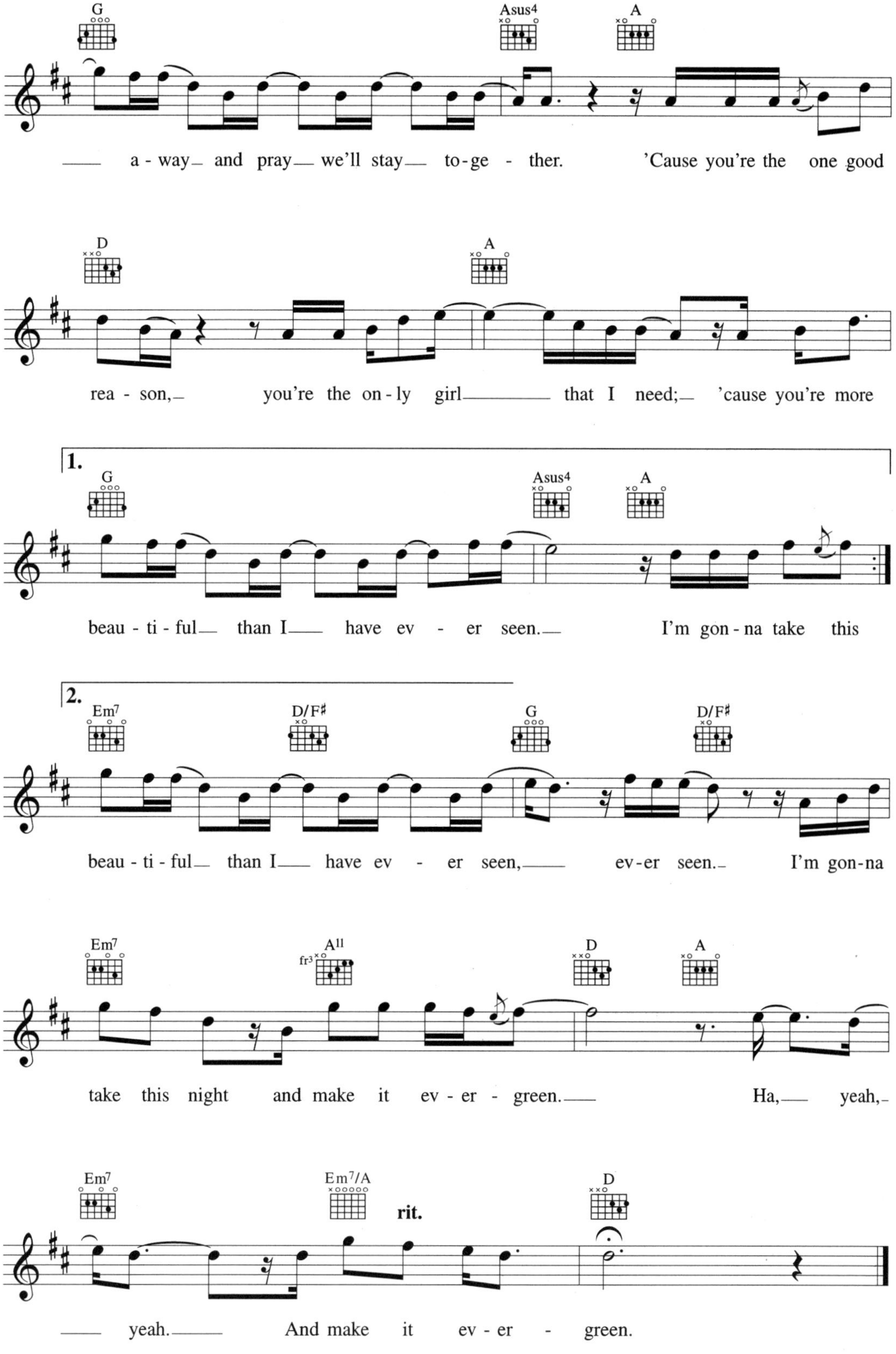
G
Asus4
A
away and pray we'll stay together. 'Cause you're the one good
D
A
reason, you're the only girl that I need; 'cause you're more
1.
G
Asus4
A
beautiful than I have ever seen. I'm gonna take this
2.
Em7
D/F♯
G
D/F♯
beautiful than I have ever seen, ever seen. I'm gonna
Em7
A11
fr3
D
A
take this night and make it evergreen. Ha, yeah,
Em7
Em7/A
rit.
D
yeah. And make it evergreen.

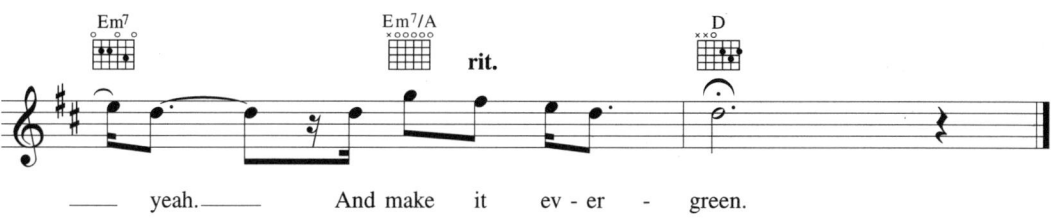

Flying Without Wings

Words & Music by Steve Mac & Wayne Hector

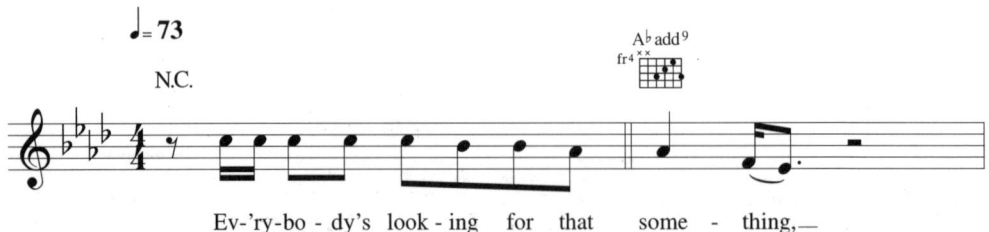

Ev-'ry-bo - dy's look - ing for that some - thing,

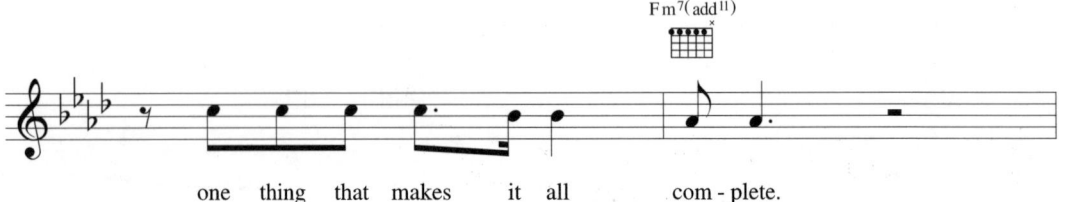

one thing that makes it all com - plete.

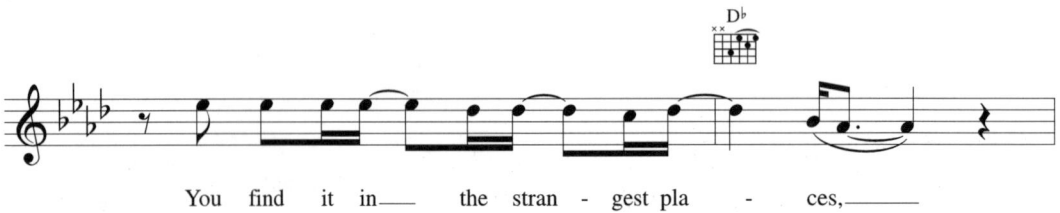

You find it in the stran - gest pla - ces,

pla - ces you nev - er knew it could be.

Some find it in the face of their child - ren,

© Copyright 1999 Rokstone Music, 21A Heathmans Road, Parsons Green, London SW6 4TJ (50%)/
Rondor Music (London) Limited, 10A Parsons Green, London SW6 4TW (50%).
All Rights Reserved. International Copyright Secured.

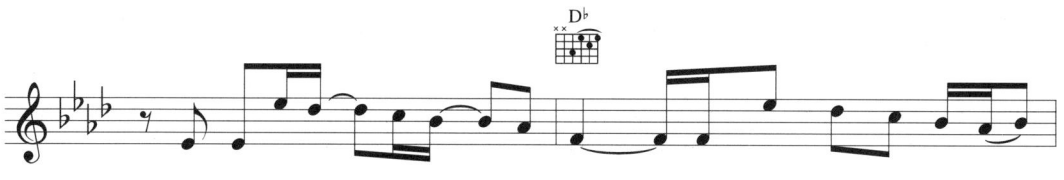
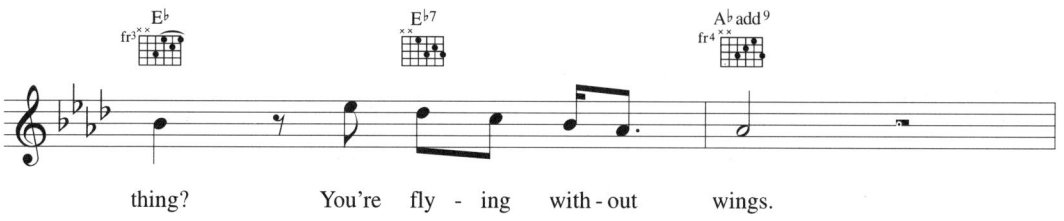

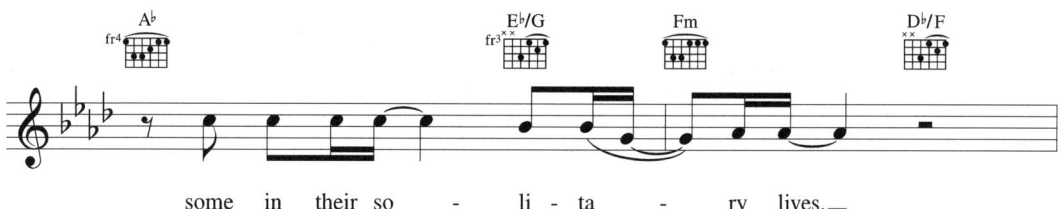
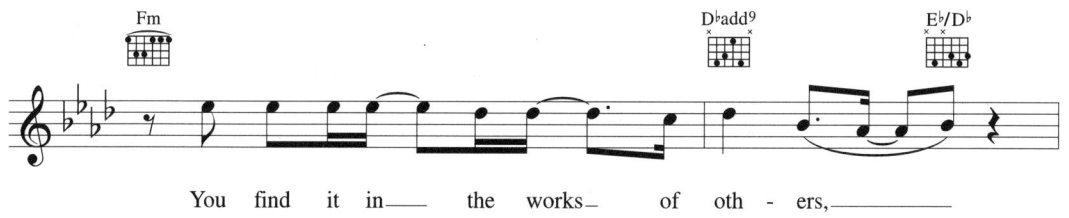

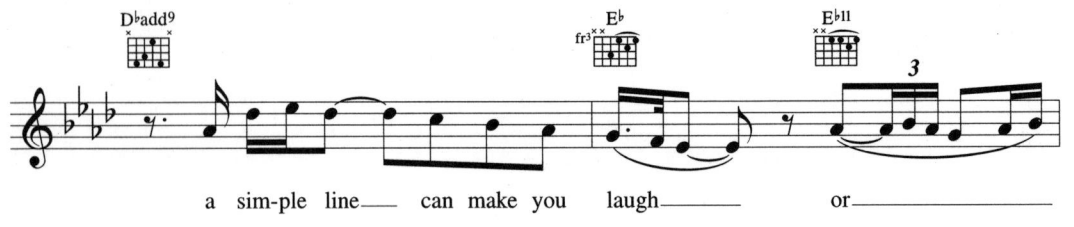
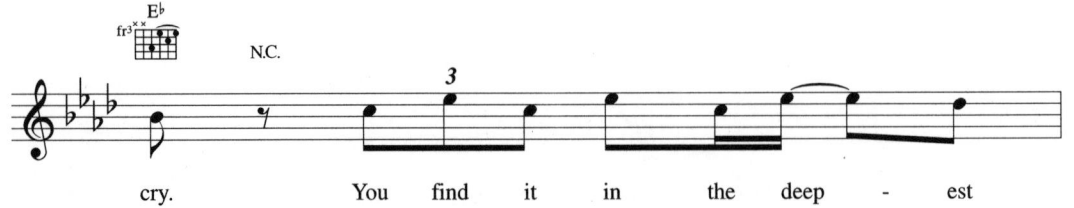
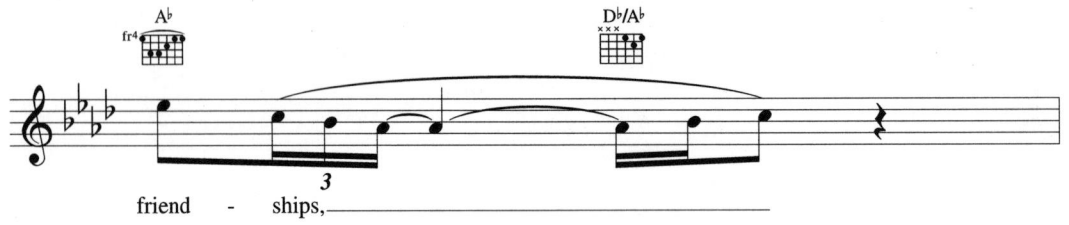
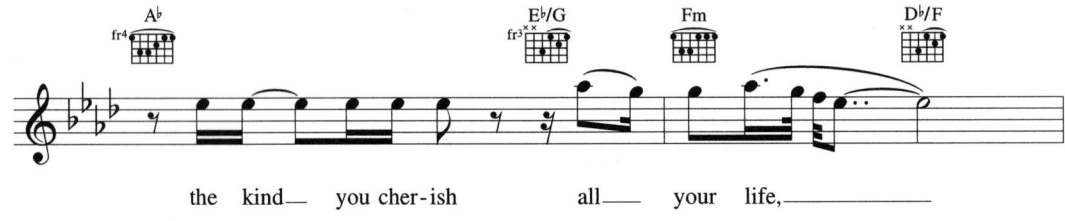

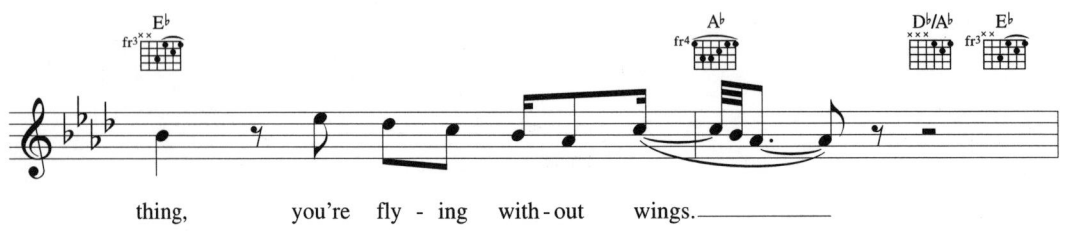

Verse 3:
Well, for me it's waking up beside you
To watch the sun rise on your face
To know that I can say I love you
At any given time or place.
It's little things that only I know
Those are the things that make you mine
And it's like flying without wings
'Cause you're my special thing
I'm flying without wings.

Unchained Melody

Words by Hy Zaret
Music by Alex North

Mack The Knife

Words by Bertolt Brecht. Music by Kurt Weill
Translation by Marc Blitzstein

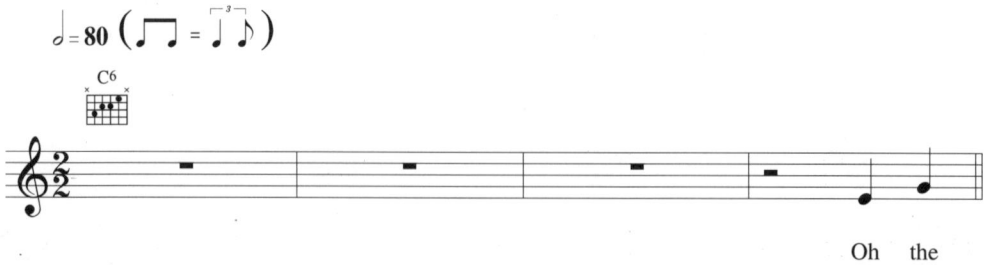

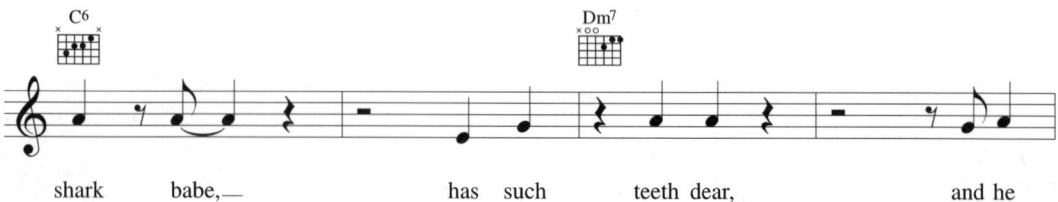

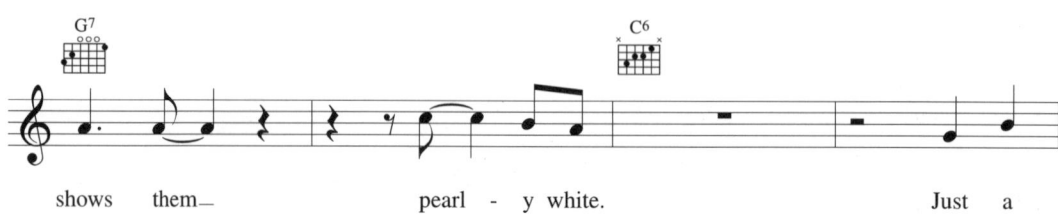

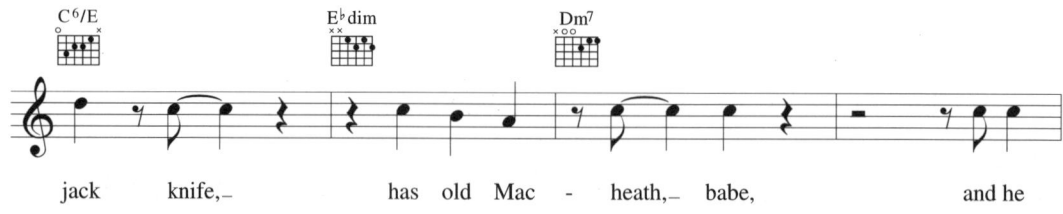

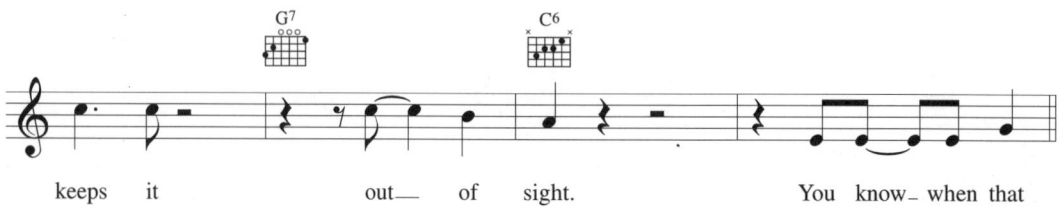

© Copyright 1928 & 1955 Universal Edition & Weill-Brecht-Harms Company Incorporated, USA.
Renewal rights assigned to The Kurt Weill Foundation for Music,
Bertolt Brecht and Edward & Josephine Davis, as Executors of the Estate of Marc Blitzstein.
Reproduced by permission of Alfred A. Kalmus Limited.
All Rights Reserved. International Copyright Secured.

E♭6 B7 E6
rash? Yeah, Jen-ny Div-er, oh Su-key
F♯m7 B7
Taw-dry, look out Miss Lot-ty Lin-ion,
E6
there's old Lu-cy Brown. Yeah the
G dim F♯m7
line forms on the right babe, now that
B7 E6 C7
Mack-ie's back in town. I said Jen-ny
F6 Gm7
Div - er - e - r, oh, Su - key Taw - - - dry,
fr3
3

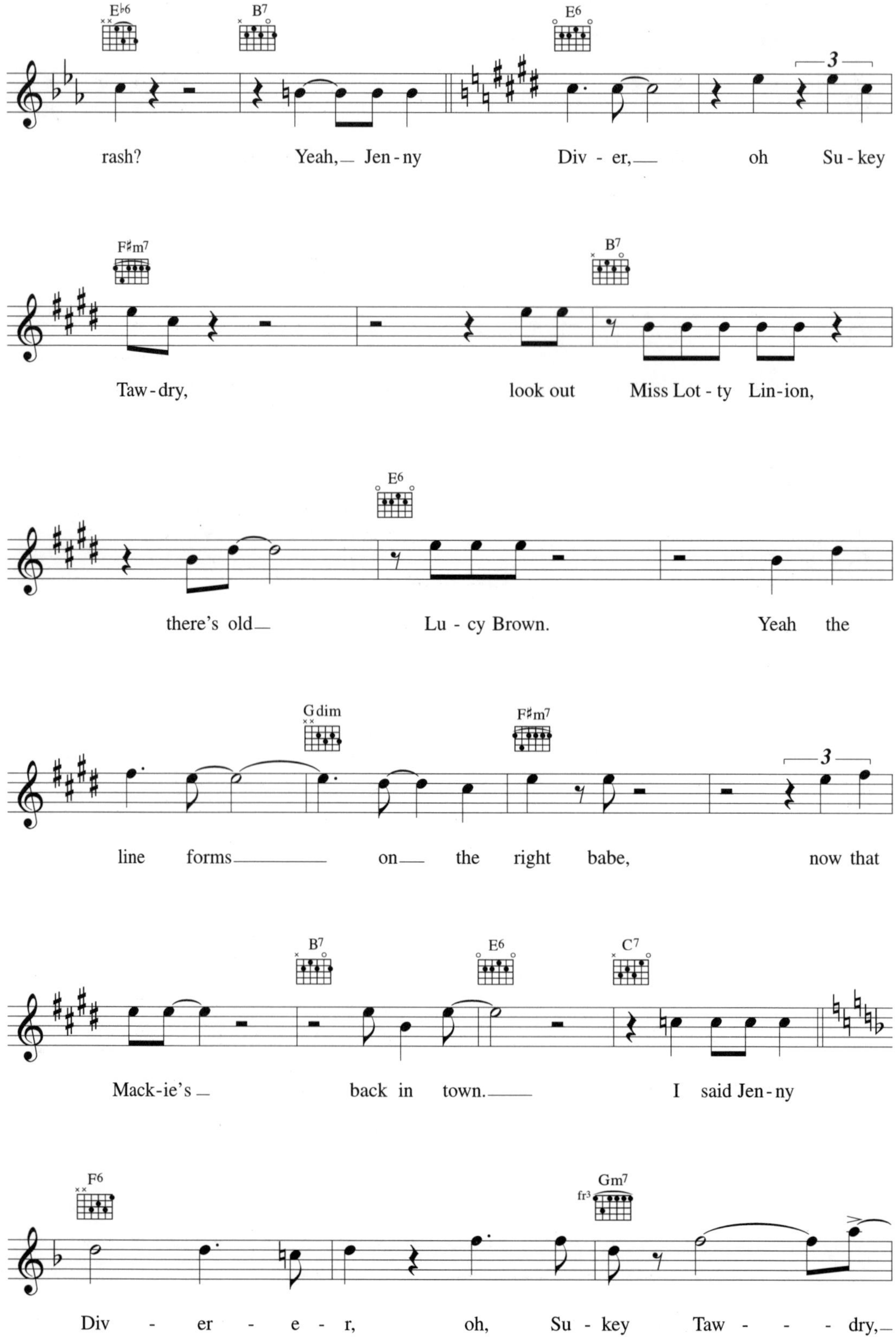

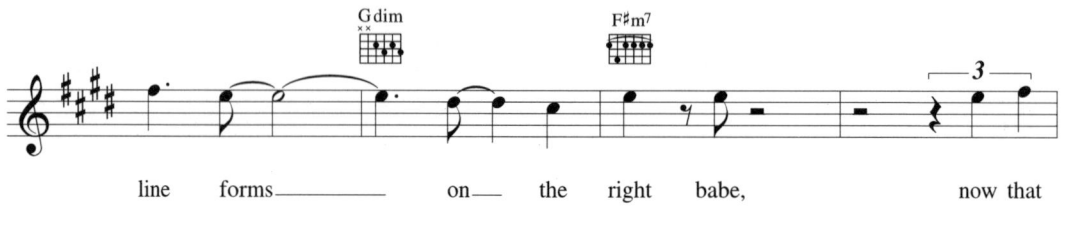

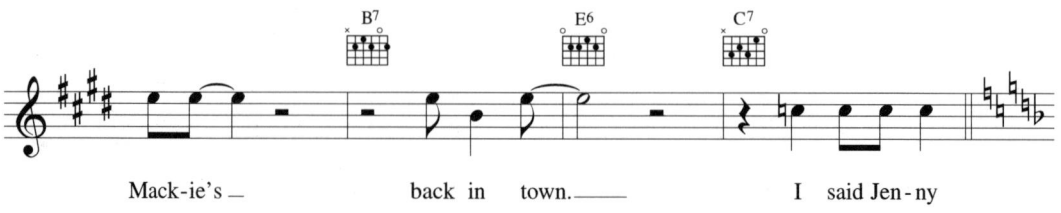

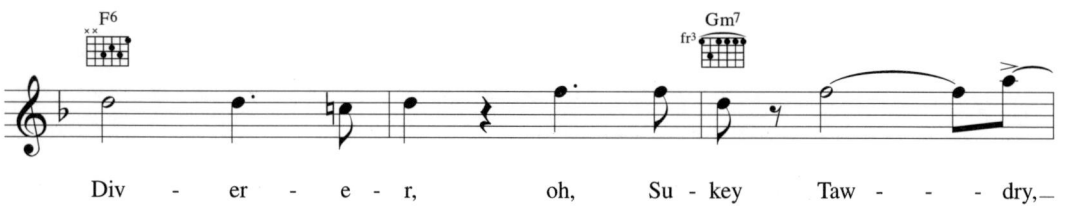

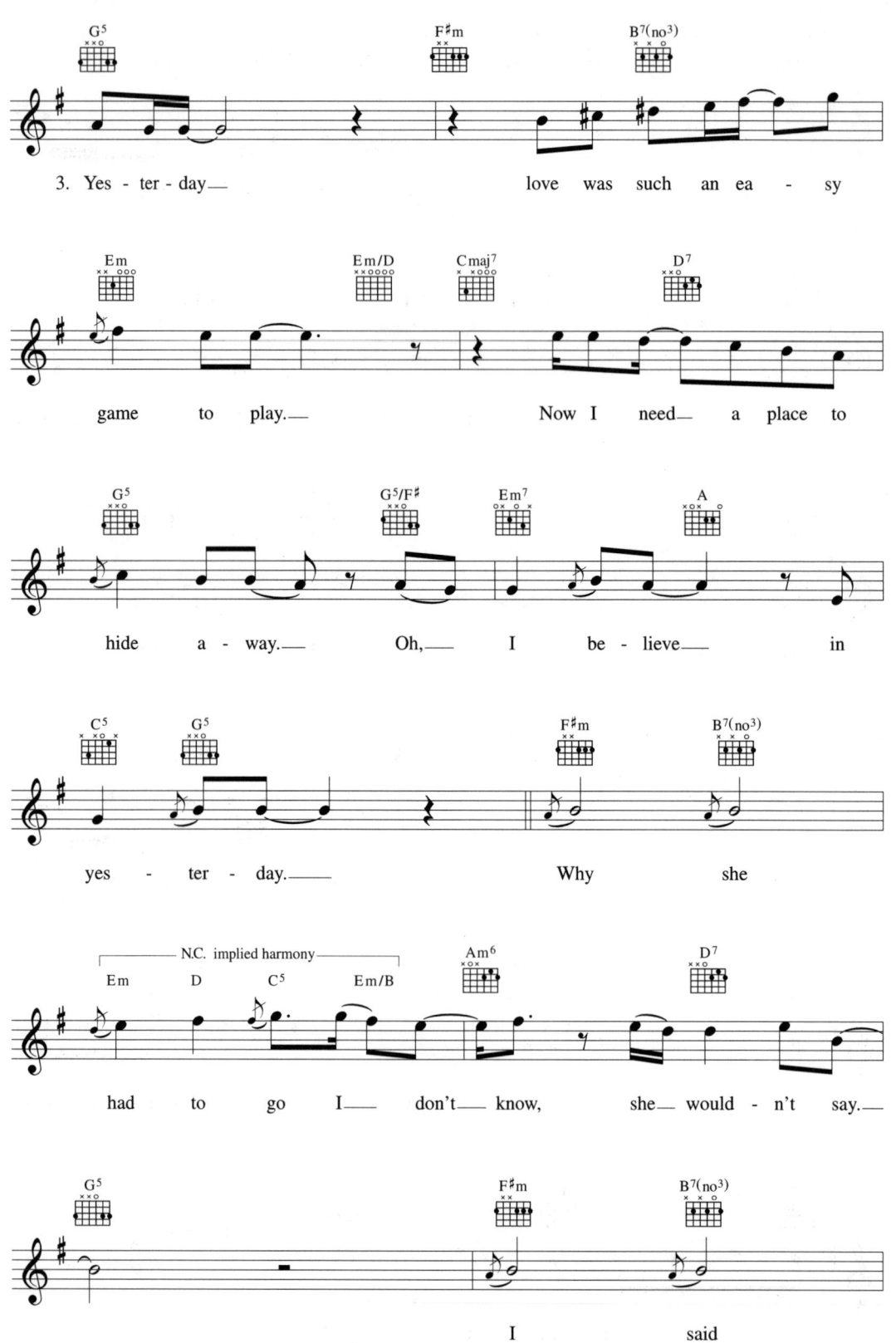

CD Track Listing

1 Evergreen (Elofsson/Magnusson/Kreuger)
BMG Music Publishing Ltd. / Peermusic (UK) Ltd. / Warner/Chappell Music Ltd.

2 Flying Without Wings (Mac/Hector)
Rokstone Music / Rondor Music (London) Ltd.

3 Unchained Melody (North/Zaret)
MPL Communications Ltd.

4 Mack The Knife (Brecht/Weill/Blitzstein)
Alfred A. Kalmus Ltd. / Universal Edition AG (Wien) / Warner/Chappell Music Ltd.

5 Yesterday (Lennon/McCartney)
Northern Songs/Sony/ATV Music Publishing (UK) Ltd.

MCPS All rights of the record producer and the owners of the works reproduced reserved. Copying, public performances and broadcasting of this recording is prohibited.

To remove your CD from the plastic sleeve, lift the small lip on the right to break the perforated flap. Replace the disc after use for convenient storage.